CLASSIC spirit

16 classic designs in
**Cashsoft Aran, Soft Tweed &
Soft Lux** by Martin Storey

Capture the Spirit of comfort in your home. Make it a place of luxury and soft colour blends. Bring interest in with the addition of texture or geometric patterns to create a focal point. In **Classic Spirit** we have created knitted accessories for the home that complement your personal look.

We are delighted to offer you three distinct themes for your home; traditional cables which cascade over a luxurious throw and bag; geometric 70's revival where circles work within squares in contrasting colours on cushions and throws; and a woven effect that brings alive subtle colour combinations in textural dimensions.

Knitting continues to be such a strong story in the home and I was so inspired, I couldn't resist carrying the themes through into cosy scarves and hats, a fun mobile phone holder and garments such as our versatile military style jacket.

Classic Spirit uses a wonderful combination of Cashsoft Aran, Soft Tweed and Soft Lux in a palette that is both rich and subtle.

I hope our designs will inspire and delight you.

Martin

The use of colour and texture in Classic Spirit makes knitting for you and your home such an enjoyable experience. Capturing the feeling of comfort and cosiness, the patterns use the softest of RYC yarn.

SIZE KEY
. . . .

■ Size 8 - 18

● Size 8 - 22

▲ Size S - XL

◆ Size S - L

✚ Accessory
(Refer to pattern page)

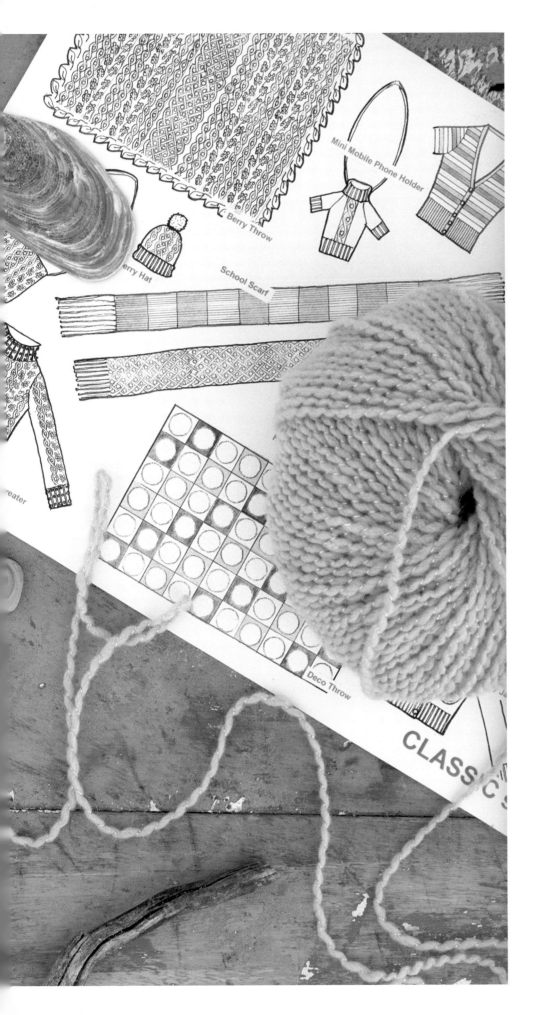

Berry Throw

Mini Mobile Phone Holder

Berry Hat

School Scarf

Sweater

Deco Throw

CLASSIC S

Cavalry jacket – Epaulettes and pocket flaps give this jacket
a military feel.

Knitted in Soft Lux, shown here in Camel. Pattern instructions page 42

Home, where my thought's escaping

Home, where my music's playing

Home, where my love lies waiting

Silently for me

Simon & Garfunkel *Homeward Bound*

Berry throw – A feast of texture in this cabled throw decorated with berry stitches and an autumn leaf trim.
Knitted in Cashsoft Aran, shown here in Sienna. Pattern instructions page 46

Berry hat – A snug cable and berry stitch hat.

Knitted in Cashsoft Aran, shown here in Aubergine. Pattern instructions page 58

School scarf – Stripes of fisherman's rib for this traditional scarf.

Knitted in Soft Lux, shown here in Powder & Clover. Pattern instructions page 55

Snowflake scarf – Extra large pompoms make this crochet-look knitted scarf very special.

Knitted in Soft Tweed, shown here in Mist. Pattern instructions page 54

Tweedy bag – Create this tweedy shopper with knitted squares of woven–look stitch.

Knitted in Soft Tweed, shown here in Thistle & Loganberry. Pattern instructions page 51

College cardigan – This multi-stripe, classic cardigan uses wonderfully muted tones.

Knitted in Soft Tweed, shown here in Loganberry, Blanket, Thistle & Mist. Pattern instructions page 36

Tweedy throw – A clever woven-look stitch
make this simple throw look so effective.

Knitted in Soft Tweed, shown here with Tweedy cushion,
both in Loganberry & Mist. Pattern instructions page 49

Berry bag – A useful satchel with lots of texture in cable and berry stitch.

Knitted in Cashsoft Aran, shown here in Mist. Pattern instructions page 56

Berry sweater – This long line cable sweater has its hem and cuffs beautifully decorated with a bobble trim.

Knitted in Cashsoft Aran, shown here in Oat. Pattern instructions page 38

When this old world starts getting me down

And people are just too much for me to face

I climb way up to the top of the stairs

And all my cares just drift right into space

On the roof, it's peaceful as can be

The Drifters *Up On The Roof*

Berry scarf – Our berry scarf is a feast of texture with wandering cables interspersed with bobbles. Knitted in Cashsoft Aran, shown here in Forest. Pattern instructions page 41

Tweedy cushion – Knit this cushion in woven-look stitch.

Tweedy cushion knitted in Soft Tweed, shown above in Kingfisher & Antique and opposite with Deco cushion in Loganberry & Mist. Pattern instructions page 53

Harvest beanie – A practical beanie adorned with autumn leaves.

Knitted in Soft Lux, shown here in Camel, Gigli & Sable. Pattern instructions page 45

Mini mobile phone holder – A sweet mobile phone holder that looks just like a mini jumper.

Knitted in Cashsoft Aran, shown here in Oat & opposite in Sienna. Pattern instructions page 59

Deco throw – A deco-inspired throw featuring circles on squares in complementary colours.
Deco cushion – Geometrically balanced, this cushion is a real talking point with the circles picked out in chain stitch.

Both knitted in Soft Lux, shown here in Mist, Camel & Sable. Pattern instructions pages 52 & 53

Tension

Obtaining the correct tension is perhaps the single factor which can make the difference between a successful garment and a disastrous one. It controls both the shape and size of an article, so any variation, however slight, can distort the finished garment. Different designers feature in our books and it is **their** tension, given at the **start** of each pattern, which you must match. We recommend that you knit a square in pattern and/or stocking stitch (depending on the pattern instructions) of perhaps 5 - 10 more stitches and 5 - 10 more rows than those given in the tension note. Mark out the central 10cm square with pins. If you have too many stitches to 10cm try again using thicker needles, if you have too few stitches to 10cm try again using finer needles. Once you have achieved the correct tension your garment will be knitted to the measurements indicated in the size diagram shown at the end of the pattern.

Sizing and Size Diagram Note

The instructions are given for the smallest size. Where they vary, work the figures in brackets for the larger sizes. **One set of figures refers to all sizes.** Included with most patterns in this magazine is a **'size diagram'**, or sketch of the finished garment and its dimensions. The size diagram shows the finished width of the garment at the under-arm point, and it is this measurement that the knitter should choose first; a useful tip is to measure one of your own garments which is a comfortable fit. Having chosen a size based on width, look at the corresponding length for that size; if you are not happy with the total length which we recommend, adjust your own garment before beginning your armhole shaping - any adjustment after this point will mean that your sleeve will not fit into your garment easily - don't forget to take your adjustment into account if there is any side seam shaping. Finally, look at the sleeve length; the size diagram shows the finished sleeve measurement, taking into account any top-arm insertion length. Measure your body between the centre of your neck and your wrist, this measurement should correspond to half the garment width plus the sleeve length. Again, your sleeve length may be adjusted, but remember to take into consideration your sleeve increases if you do adjust the length - you must increase more frequently than the pattern states to shorten your sleeve, less frequently to lengthen it.

Chart Note

Many of the patterns in the book are worked from charts. Each square on a chart represents a stitch and each line of squares a row of knitting. Each colour used is given a different letter and these are shown in the **materials** section, or in the **key** alongside the chart of each pattern. When working from the charts, read odd rows (K) from right to left and even rows (P) from left to right, unless otherwise stated.

Knitting with colour

There are two main methods of working colour into a knitted fabric: Intarsia and Fairisle techniques. The first method produces a single thickness of fabric and is usually used where a colour is only required in a particular area of a row and does not form a repeating pattern across the row, as in the fairisle technique.

Intarsia: The simplest way to do this is to cut short lengths of yarn for each motif or block of colour used in a row. Then joining in the various colours at the appropriate point on the row, link one colour to the next by twisting them around each other where they meet on the wrong side to avoid gaps. All ends can then either be darned along the colour join lines, as each motif is completed or then can be "knitted-in" to the fabric of the knitting as each colour is worked into the pattern. This is done in much the same way as "weaving-in" yarns when working the Fairisle technique and does save time darning-in ends. It is essential that the tension is noted for Intarsia as this may vary from the stocking stitch if both are used in the same pattern.

Finishing Instructions

After working for hours knitting a garment, it seems a great pity that many garments are spoiled because such little care is taken in the pressing and finishing process. Follow the following tips for a truly professional-looking garment.

Pressing

Block out each piece of knitting and following the instructions on the ball band press the garment pieces, omitting the ribs. Tip: Take special care to press the edges, as this will make sewing up both easier and neater. If the ball band indicates that the fabric is not to be pressed, then covering the blocked out fabric with a damp white cotton cloth and leaving it to stand will have the desired effect. Darn in all ends neatly along the selvedge edge or a colour join, as appropriate.

Stitching

When stitching the pieces together, remember to match areas of colour and texture very carefully where they meet. Use a seam stitch such as back stitch or mattress stitch for all main knitting seams and join all ribs and neckband with mattress stitch, unless otherwise stated.

Construction

Having completed the pattern instructions, join left shoulder and neckband seams as detailed above. Sew the top of the sleeve to the body of the garment using the method detailed in the pattern, referring to the appropriate guide:

Set-in sleeves: Place centre of cast-off edge of sleeve to shoulder seam. Set in sleeve, easing sleeve head into armhole.

Straight cast-off sleeves: Place centre of cast-off edge of sleeve to shoulder seam. Sew top of sleeve to body.

Join side and sleeve seams.
Slip stitch pocket edgings and linings into place.
Sew on buttons to correspond with buttonholes.
Ribbed welts and neckbands and any area of garter stitch should not be pressed.

Abbreviations

K	knit	sl 2	slip two stitches
P	purl	psso	pass slipped
st(s)	stitch(es)		stitch over
inc	increas(e)(ing)	tbl	through back
dec	decreas(e)(ing)		of loop
st st	stocking stitch	M1	make one stitch
	(1 row K, 1 row P)		by picking up
g st	garter stitch		horizontal loop
	(K every row)		before next stitch
beg	begin(ning)		and working into
foll	following		back of it
rem	remain(ing)	yrn	yarn round needle
rep	repeat	yfwd	yarn forward
alt	alternate	yon	yarn over needle
cont	continue	yfrn	yarn forward and
patt	pattern		round needle
tog	together	meas	measures
mm	millimetres	o	no stitches,
cm	centimetres		times, or rows
in(s)	inch(es)	-	no stitches, times
RS	right side		or rows for that
WS	wrong side		size
sl 1	slip one stitch	approx	approximately

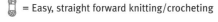 = Easy, straight forward knitting/crocheting   = Suitable for the average knitter = For the more experienced knitter

Main image page 18

College cardigan

YARN

		8	10	12	14	16	18	
To fit bust		81	86	91	97	102	107	cm
		32	34	36	38	40	42	in

Rowan RYC Soft Tweed

A	Loganberry	010	4	4	4	4	5	5	x 50gm
B	Thistle	003	2	2	2	2	2	2	x 50gm
C	Blanket	008	2	2	2	2	2	2	x 50gm
D	Mist	013	2	2	2	2	2	2	x 50gm

NEEDLES

1 pair 7mm (no 2) (US 10½) needles
1 pair 8mm (no 0) (US 11) needles
7mm (no 2) (US 10½) circular needle

BUTTONS - 5 x 00347

TENSION

12 sts and 16 rows to 10 cm measured over stocking stitch using 8mm (US 11) needles.

BACK

Using 7mm (US 10½) needles and yarn A cast on 48 [50: 52: 56: 60: 64] sts.
Row 1 (RS): K1 [0: 0: 1: 0: 1], P2 [0: 1: 2: 1: 2], *K2, P2, rep from * to last 1 [2: 3: 1: 3: 1] sts, K1 [2: 2: 1: 2: 1], P0 [0: 1: 0: 1: 0].
Row 2: P1 [0: 0: 1: 0: 1], K2 [0: 1: 2: 1: 2], rep from * to last 1 [2: 3: 1: 3: 1] sts, P1 [2: 2: 1: 2: 1], K0 [0: 1: 0: 1: 0].
These 2 rows form rib.
Work in rib for a further 22 rows, ending with RS facing for next row.
Change to 8mm (US 11) needles.
Joining in colours as required and beg with a K row, work in striped st st as folls:
Rows 1 to 4: Using yarn B.
Rows 5 to 8: Using yarn C.
Rows 9 to 12: Using yarn D, inc 1 st at each end of first of these rows.
50 [52: 54: 58: 62: 66] sts.
Rows 13 to 16: Using yarn A.
These 16 rows form striped st st and beg side seam shaping.
Cont in striped st st, inc 1 st at each end of next and foll 8th row. 54 [56: 58: 62: 66: 70] sts.
Cont straight until back meas approx 33 [33: 32: 35: 34: 36] cm, ending after 2 [2: 4: 4: 4: 2] rows

using yarn B [B: A: B: B: C] and with RS facing for next row.
Shape armholes
Keeping stripes correct, cast off 3 sts at beg of next 2 rows. 48 [50: 52: 56: 60: 64] sts.
Dec 1 st at each end of next 3 [3: 3: 5: 5: 7] rows, then on foll 2 [2: 2: 2: 3: 2] alt rows.
38 [40: 42: 42: 44: 46] sts.
Cont straight until armhole meas 20 [20: 21: 21: 22: 22] cm, ending with RS facing for next row.
Shape shoulders and back neck
Cast off 3 [4: 4: 4: 4: 4] sts at beg of next 2 rows.
32 [32: 34: 34: 36: 38] sts.
Next row (RS): Cast off 3 [4: 4: 4: 4: 4] sts, K until there are 7 [6: 7: 7: 7: 8] sts on right needle and turn, leaving rem sts on a holder.
Work each side of neck separately.
Cast off 3 sts at beg of next row.
Cast off rem 4 [3: 4: 4: 4: 5] sts.
With RS facing, rejoin appropriate yarn to rem sts, cast off centre 12 [12: 12: 12: 14: 14] sts, K to end.
Complete to match first side, reversing shapings.

LEFT FRONT

Using 7mm (US 10½) needles and yarn A cast on 25 [26: 27: 29: 31: 33] sts.
Row 1 (RS): K1 [0: 0: 1: 0: 1], P2 [0: 1: 2: 1: 2], *K2, P2, rep from * to last 2 sts, K2.
Row 2: *P2, K2, rep from * to last 1 [2: 3: 1: 3: 1] sts, P1 [2: 2: 1: 2: 1], K0 [0: 1: 0: 1: 0].
These 2 rows form rib.
Work in rib for a further 22 rows, ending with RS facing for next row.
Change to 8mm (US 11) needles.
Joining in colours as required and beg with a K row, work in striped st st as given for back, inc 1 st at beg of 9th and every foll 8th row until there are 28 [29: 30: 32: 34: 36] sts.
Cont straight until 4 rows less have been worked than on back to beg of armhole shaping, ending with RS facing for next row.
Shape front slope
Keeping stripes correct, dec 1 st at end of next and foll alt row. 26 [27: 28: 30: 32: 34] sts.
Work 1 row.
Shape armholes
Keeping stripes correct, cast off 3 sts at beg and dec 1 st at end of next row.

22 [23: 24: 26: 28: 30] sts.
Work 1 row.
Dec 1 st at armhole edge of next 3 [3: 3: 5: 5: 7] rows, then on foll 2 [2: 2: 2: 3: 2] alt rows **and at same time** dec 1 st at front slope edge of next [next: 3rd: 3rd: 3rd: 3rd] and every foll 4th row.
15 [16: 17: 17: 17: 18] sts.
Dec 1 st at front slope edge only of 2nd [2nd: 4th: 2nd: 4th: 4th] and every foll 4th row until 10 [11: 12: 12: 12: 13] sts rem.
Cont straight until left front matches back to beg of shoulder shaping, ending with RS facing for next row.
Shape shoulder
Cast off 3 [4: 4: 4: 4: 4] sts at beg of next and foll alt row.
Work 1 row.
Cast off rem 4 [3: 4: 4: 4: 5] sts.

RIGHT FRONT

Using 7mm (US 10½) needles and yarn A cast on 25 [26: 27: 29: 31: 33] sts.
Row 1 (RS): *K2, P2, rep from * to last 1 [2: 3: 1: 3: 1] sts, K1 [2: 2: 1: 2: 1], P0 [0: 1: 0: 1: 0].
Row 2: P1 [0: 0: 1: 0: 1], K2 [0: 1: 2: 1: 2], *P2, K2, rep from * to last 2 sts, P2.
These 2 rows form rib.
Work in rib for a further 22 rows, ending with RS facing for next row.
Change to 8mm (US 11) needles.
Joining in colours as required and beg with a K row, work in striped st st as given for back, inc 1 st at end of 9th and every foll 8th row until there are 28 [29: 30: 32: 34: 36] sts.
Complete to match left front, reversing shapings.

SLEEVES

Using 7mm (US 10½) needles and yarn A cast on 28 [28: 30: 30: 30: 30] sts.
Row 1 (RS): P1 [1: 2: 2: 2: 2], *K2, P2, rep from * to last 3 [3: 0: 0: 0: 0] sts, (K2, P1) 1 [1: 0: 0: 0: 0] times.
Row 2: K1 [1: 2: 2: 2: 2], *P2, K2, rep from * to last 3 [3: 0: 0: 0: 0] sts, (P2, K1) 1 [1: 0: 0: 0: 0] times.
These 2 rows form rib.
Work in rib for a further 14 rows, ending with RS facing for next row.
Change to 8mm (US 11) needles.

Joining in colours as required, beg with a K row and patt row 11 [11: 7: 11: 9: 11], work in striped st st as given for back, shaping sides by inc 1 st at each end of 7th [7th: 7th: 7th: 5th: 5th] and every foll 8th [8th: 8th: 8th: 6th: 6th] row to 40 [40: 40: 40: 34: 34] sts, then on every foll - [-: 10th: 10th: 8th: 8th] row until there are – [-: 42: 42: 44: 44] sts. Cont straight until sleeve meas approx 43 [43: 44: 44: 45: 45] cm, ending after 2 [2: 4: 4: 4: 2] rows using yarn B [B: A: B: B: C] and with RS facing for next row.

Shape top

Keeping stripes correct, cast off 3 sts at beg of next 2 rows.

34 [34: 36: 36: 38: 38] sts.

Dec 1 st at each end of next 3 rows, then on foll 2 alt rows, then on every foll 4th row until 20 [20: 22: 22: 24: 24] sts rem.

Work 1 row.

Dec 1 st at each end of next and every foll alt row to 14 sts, then on foll row, ending with RS facing for next row.

Cast off rem 12 sts.

MAKING UP

Press as described on the information page.

Join both shoulder seams using back stitch, or mattress stitch if preferred.

Front band

With RS facing, using 7mm (US 10½) circular needle and yarn A, beg and ending at cast-on edges, pick up and knit 46 [46: 45: 49: 47: 50] sts up right front opening edge to beg of front slope shaping, 40 [40: 41: 41: 42: 43] sts up right front slope, 18 [18: 18: 18: 20: 20] sts from back, 40 [40: 41: 41: 42: 43] sts down left front slope to beg of front slope shaping, then 46 [46: 45: 49: 47: 50] sts down left front opening edge.

190 [190: 190: 198: 198: 206] sts.

Row 1 (WS): P2, *K2, P2, rep from * to end.

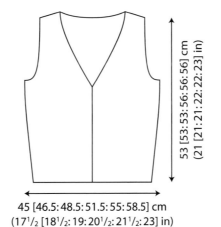

45 [46.5: 48.5: 51.5: 55: 58.5] cm
(17½ [18½: 19: 20½: 21½: 23] in)

Row 2: K2, *P2, K2, rep from * to end.

These 2 rows form rib.

Work in rib for 1 row more, ending with RS facing for next row.

Row 4 (RS): Rib 4, (work 2 tog, yrn, rib 6) twice, (work 2 tog, rib 10 [10: 10: 11: 10: 12]) twice, work 2 tog, yrn, rib to end.

Work in rib for 1 row more, ending with RS facing for next row.

Cast off in rib.

See information page for finishing instructions, setting in sleeves using the set-in method.

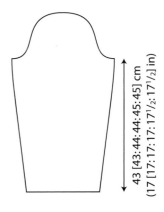

53 [53: 53: 56: 56: 56] cm
(21 [21: 21: 22: 22: 23] in)

43 [43: 44: 44: 45: 45] cm
(17 [17: 17: 17: 17½: 17½] in)

Main image page 24

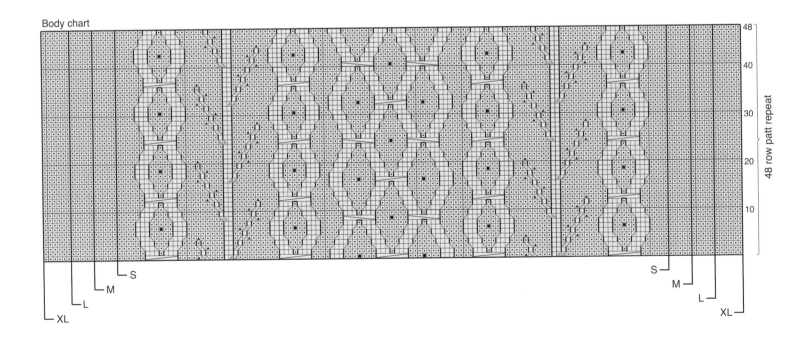

Berry sweater

YARN

	S	M	L	XL
To fit bust	81-86	91-97	102-107	112-117 cm
	32-34	36-38	40-42	44-46 in

Rowan RYC Cashsoft Aran

	19	21	23	25	x 50gm

(photographed in Oat 001)

NEEDLES

1 pair 4mm (no 8) (US 6) needles
1 pair 4½mm (no 7) (US 7) needles
Cable needle

TENSION

19 sts and 25 rows to 10 cm measured over stocking stitch using 4½mm (US 7) needles.

SPECIAL ABBREVIATIONS

Cr2R = slip next st onto cable needle and leave at back of work, K1, then P1 from cable needle;
Cr2L = slip next st onto cable needle and leave at front of work, P1, then K1 from cable needle;
C2B = slip next st onto cable needle and leave at back of work, K1 tbl, then K1 tbl from cable needle;
C2F = slip next st onto cable needle and leave at front of work, K1 tbl, then K1 tbl from cable needle;
Cr4R = slip next st onto cable needle and leave at back of work, K3, then P1 from cable needle;
Cr4L = slip next 3 sts onto cable needle and leave at front of work, P1, then K3 from cable needle; **C7B** = slip next 4 sts onto cable needle and leave at back of work, K3, slip last st on cable needle (this is centre st of original 7 sts) back onto left needle and P this st, then K3 from cable needle; **C7F** = slip next 4 sts onto cable needle and leave at front of work, K3, slip last st on cable needle (this is centre st of original 7 sts) back onto left needle and P this st, then K3 from cable needle; **MB** = (K1, P1, K1, P1, K1) all into next st, turn, P5, turn, K5, turn, P2tog, P1, P2tog, turn, sl 1, K2tog, psso;
MK = (K1, P1, K1, P1, K1) all into next st, turn, P5, turn, lift 2nd, 3rd, 4th and 5th sts on left needle over first st and off left needle, K1 tbl.

BACK

Using 4mm (US 6) needles cast on 129 [141: 153: 165] sts.
Row 1 (RS): P3, *K3, P3, rep from * to end.
Row 2: K3, *P3, K3, rep from * to end.
Rows 3 and 4: As rows 1 and 2.
Row 5: P3, *K1, MK, K1, P3, rep from * to end.
Row 6: As row 2.
These 6 rows form fancy rib.
Work in fancy rib for a further 17 rows, ending with **WS** facing for next row.
Row 24 (WS): Rib 5 [3: 4: 3], work 2 tog, (rib 11 [10: 9: 10], work 2 tog) 9 [11: 13: 13] times, rib to end.
119 [129: 139: 151] sts.
Change to 4½mm (US 7) needles.
Beg and ending rows as indicated and repeating the 48 row patt repeat throughout, work in patt from chart for body as folls:

Body chart

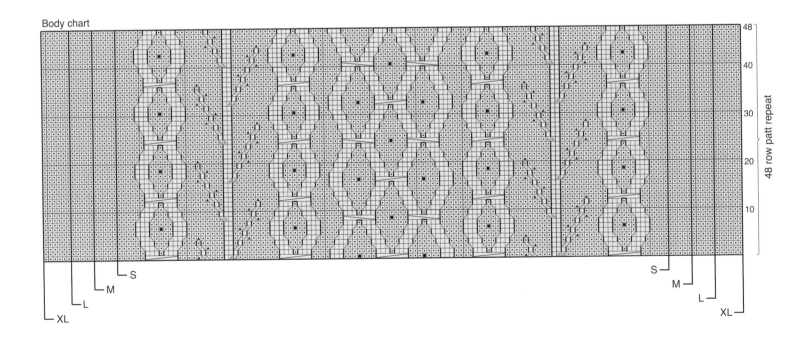

Work straight until back meas 42 [43: 44: 45] cm, ending with RS facing for next row.

Shape armholes
Keeping patt correct, cast off 6 [7: 8: 9] sts at beg of next 2 rows.
107 [115: 123: 133] sts.
Dec 1 st at each end of next 5 [7: 9: 11] rows, then on foll 3 [3: 2: 2] alt rows, then on foll 4th row.
89 [93: 99: 105] sts.
Cont straight until armhole meas 22 [23: 24: 25] cm, ending with RS facing for next row.

Shape shoulders and back neck
Cast off 7 [8: 9: 10] sts at beg of next 2 rows.
75 [77: 81: 85] sts.
Next row (RS): Cast off 7 [8: 9: 10] sts, patt until there are 12 [12: 12: 13] sts on right needle and turn, leaving rem sts on a holder.
Work each side of neck separately.
Cast off 4 sts at beg of next row.
Cast off rem 8 [8: 8: 9] sts.
With RS facing, rejoin yarn to rem sts, cast off centre

37 [37: 39: 39] sts dec 9 sts evenly, patt to end.
Complete to match first side, reversing shapings.

FRONT
Work as given for back until 16 [16: 18: 18] rows less have been worked than on back to beg of shoulder shaping, ending with RS facing for next row.

Shape neck
Next row (RS): Patt 31 [33: 36: 39] sts and turn, leaving rem sts on a holder.
Work each side of neck separately.
Keeping patt correct, dec 1 st at neck edge of next 4 rows, then on foll 5 [5: 6: 6] alt rows.
22 [24: 26: 29] sts.
Work 1 row, ending with RS facing for next row.

Shape shoulder
Cast off 7 [8: 9: 10] sts at beg of next and foll alt row.
Work 1 row.
Cast off rem 8 [8: 8: 9] sts.

With RS facing, rejoin yarn to rem sts, cast off centre 27 sts dec 4 sts evenly, patt to end.
Complete to match first side, reversing shapings.

SLEEVES
Using 4mm (US 6) needles cast on 63 [63: 69: 69] sts.
Work in fancy rib as given for back for 23 rows, ending with **WS** facing for next row.
Row 24 (WS): Rib 2 [3: 3: 3], work 2 tog, (rib 5 [7: 4: 4], work 2 tog) 8 [6: 10: 10] times, rib to end.
54 [56: 58: 58] sts.
Change to 4½mm (US 7) needles.
Beg and ending rows as indicated and repeating the 48 row patt repeat throughout, work in patt from chart for sleeve, shaping sides by inc 1 st at each end of 7th [7th: 5th: 5th] and every foll 8th [8th: 6th: 6th] row to 66 [76: 64: 80] sts, then on every foll 10th [-: 8th: 8th] row until there are 72 [-: 80: 84] sts, taking inc sts into rev st st.
Cont straight until sleeve meas 45 [46: 47: 47] cm,

Key
☐ K on RS,
P on WS

⊡ P on RS,
K on WS

▱▱ C7B

▱▱ C7F

▱▱ Cr4R

▱▱ Cr4L

▨ C2B

▨ C2F

▨ Cr2R

▨ Cr2L

▪ MB

▲ MK

Sleeve chart

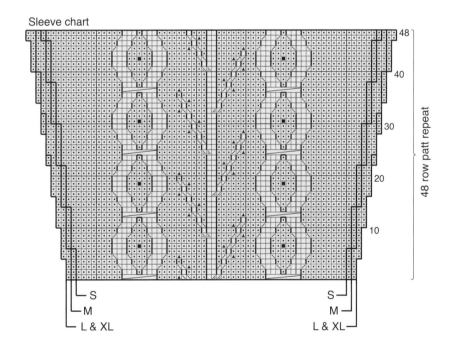

48 row patt repeat

S
M
L & XL

S
M
L & XL

ending with RS facing for next row.

Shape top

Keeping patt correct, cast off 6 [7: 8: 9] sts at beg
of next 2 rows. 60 [62: 64: 66] sts.

Dec 1 st at each end of next 5 rows, then on foll
3 alt rows, then on every foll 4th row until 36 [38:
40: 42] sts rem.

Work 1 row.

Dec 1 st at each end of next and every foll alt row
to 26 sts, then on foll row, ending with RS facing
for next row.

Cast off rem 24 sts dec 4 sts evenly.

MAKING UP

Press as described on the information page.
Join right shoulder seam using back stitch, or
mattress stitch if preferred.

Neckband

With RS facing and using 4mm (US 6) needles,
pick up and knit 23 [23: 25: 25] sts down left side
of neck, 22 sts from front, 23 [23: 25: 25] sts up
right side of neck, then 37 [37: 39: 39] sts from

back. 105 [105: 111: 111] sts.

Beg with row 2, work in fancy rib as given for back
for 24 rows, ending with **WS** facing for next row.

Cast off knitwise (on **WS**).

See information page for finishing instructions,
setting in sleeves using the set-in method.

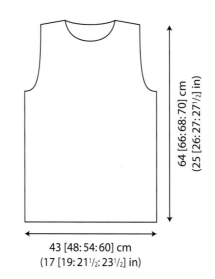

64 [66: 68: 70] cm
(25 [26: 27: 27½] in)

43 [48: 54: 60] cm
(17 [19: 21½: 23½] in)

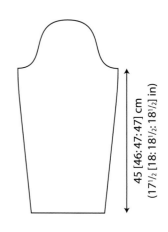

45 [46: 47: 47] cm
(17½ [18: 18½: 18½] in)

Main image page 26

 Berry scarf

YARN
Rowan RYC Cashsoft Aran
12 x 50gm
(photographed in Forest 018)

NEEDLES
1 pair 4mm (no 8) (US 6) needles
1 pair 4½mm (no 7) (US 7) needles
Cable needle

TENSION
19 sts and 25 rows to 10 cm measured over
stocking stitch using 4½mm (US 7) needles.

FINISHED SIZE
Completed scarf measures 16 cm (6¼in) wide and
232 cm (91½in) long, excluding fringe.

SPECIAL ABBREVIATIONS
C7B = slip next 4 sts onto cable needle and leave
at back of work, K3, slip centre st of these 7 sts
back onto left needle and P this st, then K3 from
cable needle;
C7F = slip next 4 sts onto cable needle and leave
at front of work, K3, slip centre st of these 7 sts

back onto left needle and P this st, then K3 from
cable needle;
Cr4R = slip next st onto cable needle and leave at
back of work, K3, then P1 from cable needle;
Cr4L = slip next 3 sts onto cable needle and
leave at front of work, P1, then K3 from cable
needle; **MB** = (K1, P1, K1, P1, K1) all into next st,
turn, P5, turn, K5, turn, P2tog, P1, P2tog, turn, sl
1, K2tog, psso.

SCARF
Using 4mm (US 6) needles cast on 45 sts.
Work in g st for 3 rows, ending with **WS** facing for
next row.
Row 4 (WS): (K3, M1) 14 times, K3.
59 sts.
Change to 4½mm (US 7) needles.
Cont in patt as folls:
Row 1 (RS): P2, K3, (P3, MB, P3, C7B) 3 times,
P3, MB, P3, K3, P2.
Row 2: K2, P3, K7, (P3, K1, P3, K7) 3 times, P3, K2.
Row 3: P2, (Cr4L, P5, Cr4R, P1) 4 times, P1.
Row 4: K1, (K2, P3, K5, P3, K1) 4 times, K2.
Row 5: P2, (P1, Cr4L, P3, Cr4R, P2) 4 times, P1.
Row 6: K1, (K3, P3, K3, P3, K2) 4 times, K2.

Row 7: P2, (P2, Cr4L, P1, Cr4R, P3) 4 times, P1.
Row 8: K1, (K4, P3, K1, P3, K3) 4 times, K2.
Row 9: P2, (P3, C7F, P3, MB) 3 times, P3, C7F, P5.
Row 10: As row 8.
Row 11: P2, (P2, Cr4R, P1, Cr4L, P3) 4 times, P1.
Row 12: As row 6.
Row 13: P2, (P1, Cr4R, P3, Cr4L, P2) 4 times, P1.
Row 14: As row 4.
Row 15: P2, (Cr4R, P5, Cr4L, P1) 4 times, P1.
Row 16: As row 2.
These 16 rows form patt.
Cont in patt until scarf meas 230 cm, ending with
RS facing for next row.
Next row (RS): (K2, K2tog) 14 times, K3. 45 sts.
Change to 4mm (US 6) needles.
Work in g st for 4 rows, ending with **WS** facing for
next row.
Cast off knitwise (on **WS**).

MAKING UP
Press as described on the information page.
Cut 60 cm lengths of yarn and knot groups of 6 of
these lengths through cast-on and cast-off edge
to form fringe, placing 11 knots evenly spaced
along each edge.

Main image page 10

Cavalry jacket

YARN

	8	10	12	14	16	18	20	22	
To fit bust	81	86	91	97	102	107	112	117	cm
	32	34	36	38	40	42	44	46	in

Rowan RYC Soft Lux

| 8 | 8 | 9 | 9 | 10 | 10 | 11 | 11 | x 50gm |

(photographed in Camel 011)

NEEDLES

1 pair 4mm (no 8) (US 6) needles
1 pair 4½mm (no 7) (US 7) needles

BUTTONS – 12 x 00339

TENSION

19 sts and 25 rows to 10 cm measured over
stocking stitch using 4½mm (US 7) needles.

BACK

Using 4mm (US 6) needles cast on 73 [77: 81: 87:
93: 97: 103: 109] sts.
Row 1 (RS): P1, *K1, P1, rep from * to end.
Row 2: K1, *P1, K1, rep from * to end.
These 2 rows form rib.
Work in rib for a further 16 rows, ending with RS
facing for next row.
Change to 4½mm (US 7) needles.
Beg with a K row, work in st st, inc 1 st at each
end of 11th and every foll 10th row until there are
83 [87: 91: 97: 103: 107: 113: 119] sts.
Cont straight until back meas 31 [31: 30: 33: 32:
34: 33: 35] cm, ending with RS facing for next row.
Shape armholes
Cast off 4 [5: 5: 6: 6: 7: 7: 8] sts at beg of next
2 rows. 75 [77: 81: 85: 91: 93: 99: 103] sts.
Dec 1 st at each end of next 3 [3: 3: 5: 5: 5: 7: 7]
rows, then on foll 3 [3: 4: 3: 4: 4: 3: 4] alt rows,
then on foll 4th row.
61 [63: 65: 67: 71: 73: 77: 79] sts.
Cont straight until armhole meas 20 [20: 21: 21: 22:
22: 23: 23] cm, ending with RS facing for next row.
Shape shoulders and back neck
Cast off 5 [6: 6: 6: 7: 7: 8: 8] sts at beg of next
2 rows. 51 [51: 53: 55: 57: 59: 61: 63] sts.
Next row (RS): Cast off 5 [6: 6: 6: 7: 7: 8: 8] sts,

K until there are 10 [9: 10: 11: 10: 11: 11: 12] sts on
right needle and turn, leaving rem sts on a holder.
Work each side of neck separately.
Cast off 4 sts at beg of next row.
Cast off rem 6 [5: 6: 7: 6: 7: 7: 8] sts.
With RS facing, rejoin yarn to rem sts, cast off
centre 21 [21: 21: 21: 23: 23: 23: 23] sts, K to end.
Complete to match first side, reversing shapings.

LOWER FLAPS (make 2)

Using 4mm (US 6) needles cast on 43 [43: 44: 44:
45: 45: 46: 46] sts.
Work in g st for 3 rows, ending with **WS** facing for
next row.
Row 4 (WS): Cast off 12 sts knitwise, K to last
12 sts, cast off rem 12 sts knitwise.
19 [19: 20: 20: 21: 21: 22: 22] sts.
Break yarn.
Change to 4½ (US 7) needles.
Rejoin yarn to sts with RS facing and, beg with a
K row, work in st st as folls:
Inc 1 st at each end of next 4 rows. 27 [27: 28: 28:
29: 29: 30: 30] sts.
Work 10 rows, ending with RS facing for next row.
Break yarn and leave sts on a holder.

UPPER FLAPS (make 2)

Using 4mm (US 6) needles cast on 33 [33: 33: 34:
34: 34: 35: 35] sts.
Work in g st for 3 rows, ending with **WS** facing for
next row.
Row 4 (WS): Cast off 10 sts knitwise, K to last
10 sts, cast off rem 10 sts knitwise.
13 [13: 13: 14: 14: 14: 15: 15] sts.
Break yarn.
Change to 4½ (US 7) needles.
Rejoin yarn to sts with RS facing and, beg with a
K row, work in st st as folls:
Inc 1 st at each end of next 3 rows.
19 [19: 19: 20: 20: 20: 21: 21] sts.
Work 9 rows, ending with RS facing for next row.
Break yarn and leave sts on a holder.

LEFT FRONT

Using 4mm (US 6) needles cast on 44 [46: 48: 50:

54: 56: 58: 62] sts.
Row 1 (RS): *P1, K1, rep from * to end.
Row 2: As row 1.
These 2 rows form rib.
Work in rib for a further 15 rows, ending with **WS**
facing for next row.
Row 18 (WS): Rib 7 and slip these sts onto a
holder, rib to last 0 [0: 0: 1: 0: 0: 1: 0] st,
(inc in last st) 0 [0: 0: 1: 0: 0: 1: 0] times.
37 [39: 41: 44: 47: 49: 52: 55] sts.
Change to 4½mm (US 7) needles.
Beg with a K row, work in st st, inc 1 st at beg of
11th and foll 10th row.
39 [41: 43: 46: 49: 51: 54: 57] sts.
Work 9 rows, ending with RS facing for next row.
Place lower flap
Next row (RS): Inc in first st, K6 [8: 9: 12: 14: 16:
18: 21], holding WS of one lower flap against RS of
left front K tog first st of lower flap with next st of
front, K tog rem 26 [26: 27: 27: 28: 28: 29: 29] sts
of lower flap with next 26 [26: 27: 27: 28: 28:
29: 29] sts of front in same way, K5.
40 [42: 44: 47: 50: 52: 55: 58] sts.
Inc 1 st at beg of 10th and foll 10th row.
42 [44: 46: 49: 52: 54: 57: 60] sts.
Cont straight until left front matches back to beg
of armhole shaping, ending with RS facing for
next row.
Shape armhole
Cast off 4 [5: 5: 6: 6: 7: 7: 8] sts at beg of next
row. 38 [39: 41: 43: 46: 47: 50: 52] sts.
Work 1 row.
Dec 1 st at armhole edge of next 3 [3: 3: 5: 5: 5:
7: 7] rows, then on foll 3 [3: 4: 3: 4: 4: 3: 3] alt
rows, then on foll 4th [4th: 0: 0: 0: 0: 0: 0] row.
31 [32: 34: 35: 37: 38: 40: 42] sts.
Work 1 [1: 3: 3: 1: 1: 1: 1] rows, ending with RS
facing for next row.
Place upper flap
Next row (RS): (K2tog) 0 [0: 1: 1: 0: 0: 0: 1] times,
K7 [8: 8: 8: 12: 13: 14: 14], holding WS of one
upper flap against RS of left front K tog first st of
upper flap with next st of front, K tog rem 18 [18:
18: 19: 19: 19: 20: 20] sts of upper flap with next
18 [18: 18: 19: 19: 19: 20: 20] sts of front in same

42

way, K5. 31 [32: 33: 34: 37: 38: 40: 41] sts.
Dec 0 [0: 0: 0: 1: 1: 1: 1] st at armhole edge of
0 [0: 0: 0: 2nd: 2nd: 2nd: 4th] row.
31 [32: 33: 34: 36: 37: 39: 40] sts.
Cont straight until 15 [15: 15: 17: 17: 17: 19: 19] rows
less have been worked than on back to beg of
shoulder shaping, ending with **WS** facing for next
row.
Shape neck
Cast off 8 [8: 8: 7: 8: 8: 7: 7] sts at beg of next
row. 23 [24: 25: 27: 28: 29: 32: 33] sts.
Dec 1 st at neck edge of next 3 rows, then on foll
3 [3: 3: 3: 4: 4: 4: 5] alt rows, then on foll 4th row.
16 [17: 18: 19: 20: 21: 23: 24] sts.
Work 1 row, ending with RS facing for next row.
Shape shoulder
Cast off 5 [6: 6: 6: 7: 7: 8: 8] sts at beg of next
and foll alt row.
Work 1 row.
Cast off rem 6 [5: 6: 7: 6: 7: 7: 8] sts.

RIGHT FRONT
Using 4mm (US 6) needles cast on 44 [46: 48: 50:
54: 56: 58: 62] sts.
Row 1 (RS): *K1, P1, rep from * to end.
Row 2: As row 1.
These 2 rows form rib.
Work in rib for a further 6 rows, ending with RS
facing for next row.
Row 9 (RS): Rib 2, K2tog, yfwd (to make a
buttonhole), rib to end.
Work in rib for a further 8 rows, ending with **WS**
facing for next row.
Row 18 (WS): (Inc in first st) 0 [0: 0: 1: 0: 0: 1: 0]
times, rib to last 7 sts and turn, leaving rem 7 sts
on a holder.
37 [39: 41: 44: 47: 49: 52: 55] sts.
Change to 4½mm (US 7) needles.
Beg with a K row, work in st st, inc 1 st at end of
11th and foll 10th row.
39 [41: 43: 46: 49: 51: 54: 57] sts.
Work 9 rows, ending with RS facing for next row.
Place lower flap
Next row (RS): K5, holding WS of second lower
flap against RS of right front K tog first st of lower

flap with next st of front, K tog rem 26 [26: 27:
27: 28: 28: 29: 29] sts of lower flap with next
26 [26: 27: 27: 28: 28: 29: 29] sts of front in
same way, K6 [8: 9: 12: 14: 16: 18: 21], inc in last
st. 40 [42: 44: 47: 50: 52: 55: 58] sts.
Inc 1 st at end of 10th and foll 10th row.
42 [44: 46: 49: 52: 54: 57: 60] sts.
Cont straight until right front matches back to
beg of armhole shaping, ending with **WS** facing
for next row.
Shape armhole
Cast off 4 [5: 5: 6: 6: 7: 7: 8] sts at beg of next row.
38 [39: 41: 43: 46: 47: 50: 52] sts.
Dec 1 st at armhole edge of next 3 [3: 3: 5: 5: 5:
7: 7] rows, then on foll 3 [3: 4: 3: 4: 4: 3: 3] alt
rows, then on foll 4th [4th: 0: 0: 0: 0: 0: 0] row.
31 [32: 34: 35: 37: 38: 40: 42] sts.
Work 1 [1: 3: 3: 1: 1: 1: 1] rows, ending with RS
facing for next row.
Place upper flap
Next row (RS): K5, holding WS of second upper
flap against RS of right front K tog first st of
upper flap with next st of front, K tog rem 18 [18:
18: 19: 19: 19: 20: 20] sts of upper flap with next
18 [18: 18: 19: 19: 19: 20: 20] sts of front in same
way, K7 [8: 8: 8: 12: 13: 14: 14], (K2tog) 0 [0: 1: 1:
0: 0: 0: 1] times.
31 [32: 33: 34: 37: 38: 40: 41] sts.
Complete to match left front, reversing shapings.

SLEEVES
Using 4mm (US 6) needles cast on 47 [47: 49: 49:
51: 51: 53: 53] sts.
Work in rib as given for back for 18 rows, ending
with RS facing for next row.
Change to 4½mm (US 7) needles.
Beg with a K row, work in st st, shaping sides by
inc 1 st at each end of 11th [9th: 9th: 7th: 7th:
7th: 7th: 5th] and every foll 12th [10th: 10th: 8th:
10th: 8th: 8th: 8th] row to 61 [59: 59: 53: 69: 63:
67: 75] sts, then on every foll - [12th: 12th: 10th: -
: 10th: 10th: -] row until there are - [63: 65: 67: -:
71: 73: -] sts.
Cont straight until sleeve meas 45 [45: 46: 46: 47:
47: 46: 46] cm, ending with RS facing for next row.

Shape top
Cast off 4 [5: 5: 6: 6: 7: 7: 8] sts at beg of next
2 rows. 53 [53: 55: 55: 57: 57: 59: 59] sts.
Dec 1 st at each end of next 3 rows, then on foll
3 alt rows, then on every foll 4th row until 33 [33:
35: 35: 37: 37: 39: 39] sts rem.
Work 1 row.
Dec 1 st at each end of next and every foll alt row
to 25 sts, then on foll 3 rows, ending with RS
facing for next row.
Cast off rem 19 sts.

MAKING UP
Press as described on the information page.
Join both shoulder seams using back stitch, or
mattress stitch if preferred.
Button band
Slip 7 sts from left front holder onto 4mm (US 6)
needles and rejoin yarn with RS facing.
Cont in rib until band, when slightly stretched,
fits up left front opening edge to neck shaping,
ending with RS facing for next row.
Break yarn and leave sts on a holder.
Slip stitch band in place.
Mark positions for 6 buttons on this band – first
button to be level with buttonhole already
worked in right front, top button to come 1 cm
below neck shaping, and rem 4 buttons evenly
spaced between.
Buttonhole band
Slip 7 sts from right front holder onto 4mm (US 6)
needles and rejoin yarn with **WS** facing.
Cont in rib until band, when slightly stretched,
fits up right front opening edge to neck shaping,
with the addition of 5 buttonholes worked to
correspond with positions marked for buttons
as folls:
Buttonhole row (RS): Rib 2, K2tog, yfwd, rib 3.
When band is complete, ending with RS facing for
next row, do NOT break yarn.
Slip stitch band in place.
Collar
With RS facing and using 4mm (US 6) needles,
rib 7 sts of buttonhole band, pick up and knit
30 [30: 30: 31: 32: 32: 33: 33] sts up right side of

neck, 31 [31: 31: 31: 33: 33: 33: 33] sts from back, and 30 [30: 30: 31: 32: 32: 33: 33] sts down left side of neck, then rib 7 sts of button band.
105 [105: 105: 107: 111: 111: 113: 113] sts.
Cont in rib as set by bands until collar meas 11 cm from pick-up row.
Cast off in rib.

Epaulettes (make 2)
Using 4mm (US 6) needles cast on 9 sts.
Row 1 (RS): K2, (P1, K1) 3 times, K1.
Row 2: K1, (P1, K1) 4 times.
Rep last 2 rows until epaulette meas 9 cm, ending with **WS** facing for next row.
Next row (WS): K1, P1, P2tog tbl, K1, P2tog, P1, K1. 7 sts.
Next row: K2, sl 1, K2tog, psso, K2. 5 sts.
Next row: K1, P3tog, K1.
Next row: sl 1, K2tog, psso and fasten off.
Lay epaulette over shoulder seam, matching cast-on edge to armhole edge and sew in place at armhole edge.

See information page for finishing instructions, setting in sleeves using the set-in method and enclosing cast-on edge of epaulette in armhole seam. Sew cast-off edges of flaps to row-end edges, then sew ends of these g st strips in place on RS. Attach buttons to flaps and epaulettes as shown in photograph, attaching them through both layers.

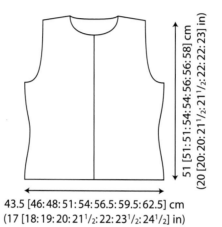

51 [51: 51: 54: 54: 56: 56: 58] cm
(20 [20: 20: 21¹/₂: 21¹/₂: 22: 22: 23] in)

43.5 [46: 48: 51: 54: 56.5: 59.5: 62.5] cm
(17 [18: 19: 20: 21¹/₂: 22: 23¹/₂: 24¹/₂] in)

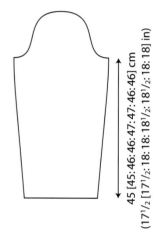

45 [45: 46: 46: 47: 47: 46: 46] cm
(17¹/₂ [17¹/₂: 18: 18: 18¹/₂: 18¹/₂: 18: 18] in)

Main image page 30

Harvest beanie

YARN

Rowan RYC Soft Lux

A Camel	011	1	x 50gm
B Sable	008	1	x 50gm
C Gigli	006	1	x 50gm

NEEDLES

1 pair 4½mm (no 7) (US 7) needles
2 double-pointed 4½mm (no 7) (US 7) needles

TENSION

19 sts and 25 rows to 10 cm measured over stocking stitch using 4½mm (US 7) needles.

HAT

Using 4½mm (US 7) needles and yarn A cast on 91 sts.
Beg with a K row, work in st st until hat meas 13 cm **allowing first few rows to roll to RS**, ending with RS facing for next row.

Shape crown
Row 1 (RS): K1, (K2tog, K8) 9 times. 82 sts.
Work 1 row.
Row 3: K1, (K2tog, K7) 9 times. 73 sts.
Work 1 row.
Row 5: K1, (K2tog, K6) 9 times. 64 sts.
Work 1 row.
Row 7: K1, (K2tog, K5) 9 times. 55 sts.
Work 1 row.
Row 9: K1, (K2tog, K4) 9 times. 46 sts.
Work 1 row.
Row 11: K1, (K2tog, K3) 9 times. 37 sts.
Work 1 row.
Row 13: K1, (K2tog, K2) 9 times. 28 sts.
Work 1 row.
Row 15: K1, (K2tog, K1) 9 times.

Break yarn and thread through rem 19 sts. Pull up tight and fasten off securely.

MAKING UP

Press as described on the information page.
Join back seam using back stitch, or mattress stitch if preferred, reversing seam for roll at cast-on edge.

First leaf
Using 4½mm (US 7) double-pointed needles and yarn B cast on 3 sts.
Next row (RS): K3, *without turning slip these 3 sts to opposite end of needle and bring yarn to opposite end of work pulling it quite tightly across back of work, K these 3 sts again, rep from * until stalk is 4 cm long.
Slip sts to opposite end of needle, with RS facing for next row.
Change to 4½mm (US 7) needles and work backwards and forwards in rows as folls:
Row 1 (RS): K1, P1, K1.
Row 2: Inc in first st, P1, inc in last st. 5 sts.
Row 3: (P1, K1) twice, P1.
Row 4: Inc in first st, K1, P1, K1, inc in last st. 7 sts.
Row 5: (K1, P1) 3 times, K1.
Row 6: Inc in first st, (P1, K1) twice, P1, inc in last st. 9 sts.
Row 7: (P1, K1) 4 times, P1.
Row 8: Inc in first st, (K1, P1) 3 times, K1, inc in last st. 11 sts.
Row 9: (K1, P1) 5 times, K1.
Row 10: Inc in first st, (P1, K1) 4 times, P1, inc in last st. 13 sts.
Row 11: Cast off 2 sts (one st on right needle), (K1, P1) 5 times. 11 sts.
Row 12: Cast off 2 sts (one st on right needle),

(K1, P1) 4 times. 9 sts.
Row 13: (P1, K1) 4 times, P1.
Rows 14 to 25: As rows 8 to 13, twice.
Row 26: P2tog, (P1, K1) twice, P1, P2tog tbl. 7 sts.
Row 27: K2tog, K1, P1, K1, sl 1, K1, psso. 5 sts.
Row 28: P2tog, P1, P2tog tbl. 3 sts.
Row 29: sl 1 purlwise, P2tog, psso and fasten off.
Cast off.

Second leaf
Using 4½mm (US 7) double-pointed needles and yarn C cast on 5 sts.
Next row (RS): K5, *without turning slip these 5 sts to opposite end of needle and bring yarn to opposite end of work pulling it quite tightly across back of work, K these 5 sts again, rep from * until stalk is 4 cm long.
Slip sts to opposite end of needle, with RS facing for next row.
Change to 4½mm (US 7) needles and work backwards and forwards in rows as folls:
Row 1 (RS): K2, yfwd, K1, yfwd, K2. 7 sts.
Row 2 and every foll alt row: Purl.
Row 3: K3, yfwd, K1, yfwd, K3. 9 sts.
Row 5: K4, yfwd, K1, yfwd, K4. 11 sts.
Row 7: K5, yfwd, K1, yfwd, K5. 13 sts.
Row 9: K6, yfwd, K1, yfwd, K6. 15 sts.
Row 11: sl 1, K1, psso, K to last 2 sts, K2tog. 13 sts.
Row 12: Purl.
Rows 13 to 22: As rows 11 and 12, 5 times. 3 sts.
Row 23: sl 1, K2tog, psso and fasten off.
Cast off.
Sew leaves to hat as in photograph – attach first leaf by working a line of back stitch centrally along leaf, leaving stalk free. Attach second leaf at fasten off point and at top of stalk, leaving rest of leaf free.

Berry throw

YARN

Rowan RYC Cashsoft Aran
65 x 50gm
(photographed in Sienna 015)

NEEDLES

1 pair 4½mm (no 7) (US 7) needles
Cable needle

TENSION

19 sts and 25 rows to 10 cm measured over
stocking stitch using 4½mm (US 7) needles.

FINISHED SIZE

Completed throw measures 167 cm (65¾in) wide
and 192 cm (75½in) long, including edging.

SPECIAL ABBREVIATIONS

Cr2R = slip next st onto cable needle and leave at
back of work, K1, then P1 from cable needle;
Cr2L = slip next st onto cable needle and leave at
front of work, P1, then K1 from cable needle;

C2B = slip next st onto cable needle and leave at
back of work, K1 tbl, then K1 tbl from cable needle;
C2F = slip next st onto cable needle and leave at
front of work, K1 tbl, then K1 tbl from cable needle;
Cr4R = slip next st onto cable needle and leave at
back of work, K3, then P1 from cable needle;
Cr4L = slip next 3 sts onto cable needle and
leave at front of work, P1, then K3 from cable
needle; **C7B** = slip next 4 sts onto cable needle
and leave at back of work, K3, slip last st on
cable needle (this is centre st of original 7 sts)
back onto left needle and P this st, then K3 from
cable needle; **C7F** = slip next 4 sts onto cable
needle and leave at front of work, K3, slip last st
on cable needle (this is centre st of original 7 sts)
back onto left needle and P this st, then K3 from
cable needle; **MB** = (K1, P1, K1, P1, K1) all into
next st, turn, P5, turn, K5, turn, P2tog, P1, P2tog,
turn, sl 1, K2tog, psso;
MK = (K1, P1, K1, P1, K1) all into next st, turn, P5,
turn, lift 2nd, 3rd, 4th and 5th sts on left needle
over first st and off left needle, K1 tbl.

CENTRE PANEL

Using 4½mm (US 7) needles cast on 143 sts.
Beg and ending rows as indicated and repeating
the 48 row patt repeat throughout, work in patt
from chart until centre panel meas 178 cm,
ending with RS facing for next row.
Cast off.

LEFT PANEL

Using 4½mm (US 7) needles cast on 153 sts.
Beg and ending rows as indicated and repeating
the 48 row patt repeat throughout, work in patt
from chart until left panel meas 178 cm, ending
with RS facing for next row.
Cast off.

RIGHT PANEL

Using 4½mm (US 7) needles cast on 153 sts.
Beg and ending rows as indicated and repeating
the 48 row patt repeat throughout, work in patt
from chart until right panel meas 178 cm, ending
with RS facing for next row.

Centre panel

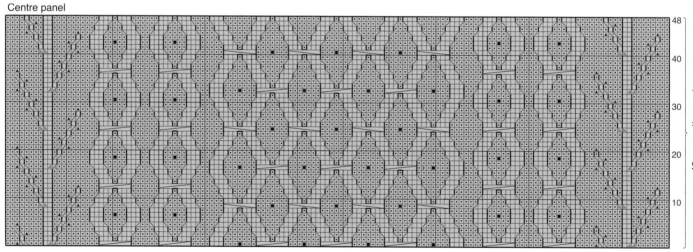

48 row patt repeat

Left panel

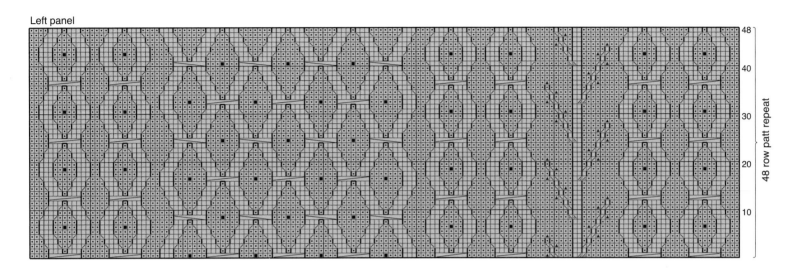

48

40

30

20

10

48 row patt repeat

Right panel

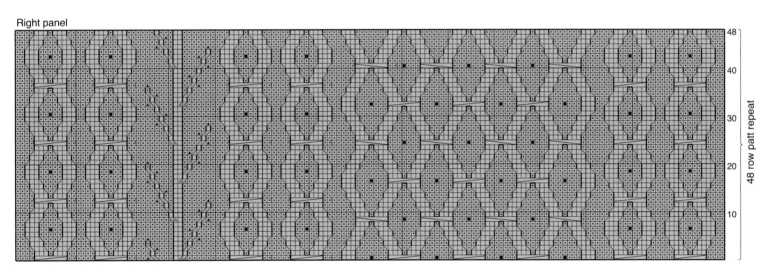

48

40

30

20

10

48 row patt repeat

Key

▫	K on RS, P on WS		▨	Cr2R
			◪	Cr2L
◩	P on RS, K on WS		▨	C2B
			◪	C2F
▱	C7B		▪	MB
▱	C7F		▲	MK
▨	Cr4R			
◪	Cr4L			

47

Cast off.

MAKING UP

Press as described on the information page. Join left and right panels to centre panel along row-end edges.

Edging

Using 4½mm (US 7) needles cast on 8 sts.

Row 1 (RS): K5, yfwd, K1, yfwd, K2. 10 sts.

Row 2: P6, inc knitwise in next st, K3. 11 sts.

Row 3: K4, P1, K2, yfwd, K1, yfwd, K3. 13 sts.

Row 4: P8, inc knitwise in next st, K4. 14 sts.

Row 5: K4, P2, K3, yfwd, K1, yfwd, K4. 16 sts.

Row 6: P10, inc knitwise in next st, K5. 17 sts.

Row 7: K4, P3, K4, yfwd, K1, yfwd, K5. 19 sts.

Row 8: P12, inc knitwise in next st, K6. 20 sts.

Row 9: K4, P4, sl 1, K1, psso, K7, K2tog, K1. 18 sts.

Row 10: P10, inc knitwise in next st, K7. 19 sts.

Row 11: K4, P5, sl 1, K1, psso, K5, K2tog, K1. 17 sts.

Row 12: P8, inc knitwise in next st, K2, P1, K5. 18 sts.

Row 13: K4, P1, K1, P4, sl 1, K1, psso, K3, K2tog, K1. 16 sts.

Row 14: P6, inc knitwise in next st, K3, P1, K5. 17 sts.

Row 15: K4, P1, K1, P5, sl 1, K1, psso, K1, K2tog, K1. 15 sts.

Row 16: P4, inc knitwise in next st, K4, P1, K5. 16 sts.

Row 17: K4, P1, K1, P6, sl 1, K2tog, psso, K1. 14 sts.

Row 18: P2tog, cast off until 7 sts rem on left needle (one st on right needle), P3, K4. 8 sts.

These 18 rows form patt.

Cont in patt until edging fits around entire outer edge of joined panels, easing it to fit around corners, ending after patt row 18 and with RS facing for next row.

Cast off.

Join cast-on and cast-off ends of edging, then slip stitch edging in place.

Main image page 20

Tweedy throw

Main image page 20

YARN
Rowan RYC Soft Tweed

A	Loganberry	010	11x 50gm
B	Mist	013	11x 50gm

NEEDLES
1 pair 7mm (no 2) (US 10½) needles
1 pair 8mm (no 0) (US 11) needles

TENSION
12 sts and 23 rows to 10 cm measured over
pattern using 8mm (US 11) needles.

FINISHED SIZE
Completed throw measures 152 cm (60 in)
square.

SPECIAL ABBREVIATIONS
wyab = with yarn at back of work (on RS rows
this will be WS of work, and on WS rows this will
be RS of work); **wyaf** = with yarn at front of work
(on RS rows this will be RS of work, and on WS
rows this will be WS of work).

Pattern note: Slip all sts knitwise on RS rows,
and purlwise on WS rows.

BLOCK A (make 2)
Using 7mm (US 10½) needles and yarn A cast on
85 sts.
Work in g st for 8 rows, ending with RS facing for
next row.
Change to 8mm (US 11) needles.
Cont in patt as folls:
Row 1 (RS): Using yarn A, knit.
Row 2: Using yarn A, purl.
Row 3: Using yarn B, K2, sl 3 wyaf, *sl 1 wyab, K1,
sl 1 wyab, sl 3 wyaf, rep from * to last 2 sts, K2.
Row 4: Using yarn B, P2, sl 3 wyab, *sl 1 wyaf, K1,
sl 1 wyaf, sl 3 wyab, rep from * to last 2 sts, P2.
Rows 5 and 6: As rows 1 and 2.
Row 7: Using yarn B, K1, (K1, sl 1 wyab) twice,
*sl 3 wyaf, sl 1 wyab, K1, sl 1 wyab, rep from * to
last 2 sts, K2.
Row 8: Using yarn B, P2, sl 1 wyaf, K1, sl 1 wyaf,
*sl 3 wyab, sl 1 wyaf, K1, sl 1 wyaf, rep from * to
last 2 sts, P2.
These 8 rows form patt.
Cont in patt for a further 158 rows, ending with
RS facing for next row.
Cast off.

BLOCK B (make 2)
Work as given for block A **but using yarn B in
place of yarn A and vice versa.**

MAKING UP
Press as described on the information page.
Join one block A to one block B along cast-off
edges. Now join pairs of joined blocks along row-
end edges, positioning block A next to block B.
Side borders (both alike)
Using 7mm (US 10½) needles and yarn A cast on
6 sts.
Work in g st until border, when slightly stretched,
fits up side of block A from cast-on edge to seam
where blocks meet, ending with RS facing for
next row.
Break off yarn A and join in yarn B.
Cont in g st until border, when slightly stretched,
fits down side of block B to cast-on edge, ending
with **WS** facing for next row.
Cast off knitwise (on **WS**).
Slip stitch borders in place.

Main image page 20

Tweedy cushion

YARN
Rowan RYC Soft Tweed

	1st colourway	2nd colourway	
A	Loganberry 010	Kingfisher 009	2 x 50gm
B	Mist 013	Antique 002	2 x 50gm

NEEDLES
1 pair 8mm (no 0) (US 11) needles

EXTRAS – piece of backing fabric 50 cm square and 46 cm square cushion pad

TENSION
12 sts and 23 rows to 10 cm measured over pattern using 8mm (US 11) needles.

FINISHED SIZE
Completed cushion cover fits 46 cm (18 in) square cushion pad snuggly.

SPECIAL ABBREVIATIONS
wyab = with yarn at back of work (on RS rows this will be WS of work, and on WS rows this will be RS of work); **wyaf** = with yarn at front of work (on RS rows this will be RS of work, and on WS rows this will be WS of work).

Pattern note: Slip all sts knitwise on RS rows, and purlwise on WS rows.

CUSHION FRONT
Using 8mm (US 11) needles and yarn A cast on 55 sts.
Row 1 (RS): Using yarn A, knit.
Row 2: Using yarn A, purl.
Row 3: Using yarn B, K2, sl 3 wyaf, *sl 1 wyab, K1, sl 1 wyab, sl 3 wyaf, rep from * to last 2 sts, K2.
Row 4: Using yarn B, P2, sl 3 wyab, *sl 1 wyaf, K1, sl 1 wyaf, sl 3 wyab, rep from * to last 2 sts, P2.
Rows 5 and 6: As rows 1 and 2.
Row 7: Using yarn B, K1, (K1, sl 1 wyab) twice, *sl 3 wyaf, sl 1 wyab, K1, sl 1 wyab, rep from * to last 2 sts, K2.
Row 8: Using yarn B, P2, sl 1 wyaf, K1, sl 1 wyaf, *sl 3 wyab, sl 1 wyaf, K1, sl 1 wyaf, rep from * to last 2 sts, P2.
These 8 rows form patt.
Cont in patt for a further 98 rows, ending with RS facing for next row.
Cast off.

MAKING UP
Press as described on the information page.
Trim backing fabric to 49 cm square – this includes 1.5 cm seam allowance along all edges. Sew knitted section to backing fabric along 3 sides, stretching knitted section slightly to fit. Insert cushion pad and sew fourth side closed.

Main image page 16

Tweedy bag

YARN
Rowan RYC Soft Tweed

A	Loganberry	010	2	x 50gm
B	Thistle	003	2	x 50gm

NEEDLES
1 pair 7mm (no 2) (US 10½) needles
1 pair 8mm (no 0) (US 11) needles

TENSION
12 sts and 23 rows to 10 cm measured over
pattern using 8mm (US 11) needles.

FINISHED SIZE
Completed bag is approx 29 cm (11½in) square.

SPECIAL ABBREVIATIONS
wyab = with yarn at back of work (on RS rows
this will be WS of work, and on WS rows this will
be RS of work);
wyaf = with yarn at front of work (on RS rows this
will be RS of work, and on WS rows this will be
WS of work).

Pattern note: Slip all sts knitwise on RS rows,
and purlwise on WS rows.

BLOCK A (make 4)
Using 8mm (US 11) needles and yarn A cast on
19 sts.
Row 1 (RS): Using yarn A, knit.
Row 2: Using yarn A, purl.
Row 3: Using yarn B, K2, sl 3 wyaf, *sl 1 wyab, K1,
sl 1 wyab, sl 3 wyaf, rep from * to last 2 sts, K2.
Row 4: Using yarn B, P2, sl 3 wyab, *sl 1 wyaf, K1,
sl 1 wyaf, sl 3 wyab, rep from * to last 2 sts, P2.
Rows 5 and 6: As rows 1 and 2.
Row 7: Using yarn B, K1, (K1, sl 1 wyab) twice,
*sl 3 wyaf, sl 1 wyab, K1, sl 1 wyab, rep from * to
last 2 sts, K2.

Row 8: Using yarn B, P2, sl 1 wyaf, K1, sl 1 wyaf,
*sl 3 wyab, sl 1 wyaf, K1, sl 1 wyaf, rep from * to
last 2 sts, P2.
These 8 rows form patt.
Cont in patt for a further 26 rows, ending with RS
facing for next row.
Cast off.

BLOCK B (make 4)
Work as given for block A **but using yarn B in
place of yarn A and vice versa**.

HANDLES (make 2)
Using 7mm (US 10½) needles and yarn B cast on
44 sts.
Work in g st for 5 rows, ending with **WS** facing for
next row.
Cast off knitwise (on **WS**).

MAKING UP
Press as described on the information page.
Join cast-off edge of first block A to cast-on edge
of first block B, then join cast-off edge of second
block B to cast-on edge of second block A. Join
pairs of joined blocks along one row-end edge –
this forms front of bag. Now join rem 4 blocks
together in same way to form back.
Upper borders (both alike)
With RS facing, using 7mm (US 10½) needles and
yarn A, pick up and knit 38 sts along cast-on
edges of front.
Work in g st for 4 rows, ending with **WS** facing for
next row.
Cast off knitwise (on **WS**).
Work upper border across top (cast-on edge)of
back in same way.
Join front and back along row-end and cast-off
edges. Using photograph as a guide, attach ends
of handles inside upper edge, positioning
handles approx 10 cm apart.

Main image page 32

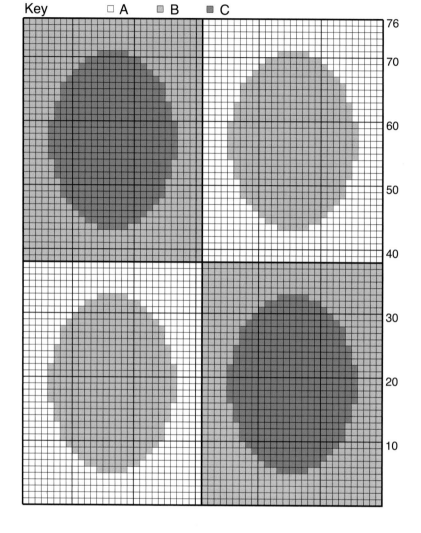

Deco throw

YARN

Rowan RYC Soft Lux

A	Mist	009	6	x 50gm
B	Camel	011	6	x 50gm
C	Sable	008	7	x 50gm

NEEDLES

1 pair 4½mm (no 7) (US 7) needles

TENSION

19 sts and 25 rows to 10 cm measured over
stocking stitch using 4½mm (US 7) needles.

FINISHED SIZE

Completed throw measures 120 cm (47¼in) wide
by 150 cm (59 in) long.

BLOCK A (make 10)

Using 4½mm (US 7) needles cast on 29 sts using
yarn A, then 29 sts using yarn B. 58 sts.
Using the **intarsia** technique as described on the
information page, work 76 rows in patt from chart,
which is worked entirely in st st beg with a K row,
ending with RS facing for next row.
Cast off.

BLOCK B (make 10)

Using 4½mm (US 7) needles cast on 29 sts using
yarn A, then 29 sts using yarn C. 58 sts.
Using yarn B in place of yarn C and yarn C in
place of yarn B and the **intarsia** technique as
described on the information page, work 76 rows
in patt from chart, which is worked entirely in st
st beg with a K row, ending with RS facing for
next row.
Cast off.

MAKING UP

Press as described on the information page.
Using photograph as a guide, outline each circle
with chain stitch – use yarn A to outline circles in
yarn B or C, yarn C to outline circles in yarn B,
and yarn B to outline circles in yarn C.

Join blocks to form one large rectangle, 4 blocks
wide and 5 blocks long, alternating blocks A and
B to create a checkerboard effect.

Main image page 28

 Deco cushion

YARN

Rowan RYC Soft Lux

	1st colourway	2nd colourway		
A	Mist 009	Mist 009	1	x 50gm
B	Camel 011	Azure 012	1	x 50gm
C	Sable 008	Ciel 004	1	x 50gm

NEEDLES

1 pair 4½mm (no 7) (US 7) needles

EXTRAS – piece of backing fabric 35 cm square
and 30 cm square cushion pad

TENSION

19 sts and 25 rows to 10 cm measured over
stocking stitch using 4½mm (US 7) needles.

FINISHED SIZE

Completed cushion measures 30 cm (12 in) square.

CUSHION FRONT

Using 4½mm (US 7) needles cast on 29 sts using
yarn A, then 29 sts using yarn B. 58 sts.
Using the **intarsia** technique as described on the
information page, work 76 rows in patt from chart
on page 52, which is worked entirely in st st beg
with a K row, ending with RS facing for next row.
Cast off.

MAKING UP

Press as described on the information page.
Using photograph as a guide, outline each circle
with chain stitch – use yarn A to outline circles in
yarn C, and yarn C to outline circles in yarn B.
Trim backing fabric to same size as knitted
section, adding seam allowance along all edges.
Sew knitted section to backing fabric along
3 sides. Insert cushion pad and sew fourth
side closed.

Main image page 16

 Snowflake scarf

YARN
Rowan RYC Soft Tweed
        5 x 50gm
(photographed in Mist 013)

NEEDLES
1 pair 8mm (no 0) (US 11) needles

TENSION
15 sts and 12 rows to 10 cm measured over
pattern using 8mm (US 11) needles.

FINISHED SIZE
Completed scarf measures 18 cm (7 in) wide and
170 cm (67 in) long, excluding pompons.

SCARF
Using 8mm (US 11) needles cast on 27 sts.

Row 1 (RS): K2, *sl 2 knitwise, lift 2nd st on right
needle over first st and off right needle,
sl 1 knitwise, lift 2nd st on right needle over first
st and off right needle, slip st on right needle
back onto left needle, (yfwd) twice, K1, rep from *
to last st, K1.
Row 2: K3, *P1, K2, rep from * to end.
These 2 rows form patt.
Cont in patt until scarf meas 170 cm, ending with
RS facing for next row.
Cast off.

MAKING UP
Press as described on the information page.
Run gathering threads along cast-on and cast-off
edges of scarf. Pull up tight and fasten off
securely. Make two 12 cm diameter pompons and
attach to gathered ends of scarf.

Main image page 14

 ## School scarf

YARN
Rowan RYC Soft Lux
A Clover   010   4 x 50gm
B Powder   002   3 x 50gm

NEEDLES
1 pair 4½mm (no 7) (US 7) needles

TENSION
19 sts and 33 rows to 10 cm measured over
pattern using 4½mm (US 7) needles.

FINISHED SIZE
Completed scarf measures 21 cm (8¼in) wide and
197 cm (77½in) long, excluding fringe.

SPECIAL ABBREVIATIONS
K1B = K next st one row below **at same time**
slipping off st above.

SCARF
Using 4½mm (US 7) needles and yarn A cast on
40 sts.

Row 1 (WS): Purl.
Cont in patt as folls:
Row 1 (RS): *P1, K1B, rep from * to last 2 sts, P2.
Row 2: As row 1.
These 2 rows form patt.
Cont in patt for a further 48 rows, ending with RS
facing for next row.
Break off yarn A and join in yarn B.
Work 50 rows in patt.
Break off yarn B and join in yarn A.
Work 50 rows in patt.
Rep last 100 rows 4 times more, then first 99 rows
again, ending after 49 rows using yarn A and with
WS facing for next row.
(Scarf should meas 197 cm.)
Cast off knitwise (on **WS**).

MAKING UP
Press as described on the information page.
Cut 60 cm lengths of yarn A and knot groups of
6 of these lengths through cast-on and cast-off
edges to form fringe, placing 10 knots evenly
spaced along each edge.

Main image page 22

Berry bag

YARN

Rowan RYC Cashsoft Aran

11 x 50gm

(photographed in Mist 016)

NEEDLES

1 pair 4mm (no 8) (US 6) needles
1 pair 4½mm (no 7) (US 7) needles
Cable needle

EXTRAS – 110 cm of 4 cm wide petersham ribbon.
Red and blue markers

TENSION

19 sts and 25 rows to 10 cm measured over
stocking stitch using 4½mm (US 7) needles.

FINISHED SIZE

Completed bag is 34 cm (13½ in) wide and 41 cm
(16 in) deep.

SPECIAL ABBREVIATIONS

C7B = slip next 4 sts onto cable needle and leave
at back of work, K3, slip centre st of these 7 sts
back onto left needle and P this st, then K3 from
cable needle;

C7F = slip next 4 sts onto cable needle and leave
at front of work, K3, slip centre st of these 7 sts
back onto left needle and P this st, then K3 from
cable needle;

Cr4R = slip next st onto cable needle and leave at
back of work, K3, then P1 from cable needle;

Cr4L = slip next 3 sts onto cable needle and leave
at front of work, P1, then K3 from cable needle;

MB = (K1, P1, K1, P1, K1) all into next st, turn, P5,
turn, K5, turn, P2tog, P1, P2tog, turn, sl 1, K2tog,
psso.

FRONT

Using 4mm (US 6) needles cast on 83 sts.
Beg and ending rows as indicated and repeating

the 48 row patt repeat throughout, work in patt
from chart until front meas 39 cm, ending with RS
facing for next row.

Next row (RS): K4, K2tog, (K2, K2tog) 18 times,
K5.

64 sts.

Change to 4mm (US 6) needles.

Work in g st for 4 rows, ending with **WS** facing for
next row.

Cast off knitwise (on **WS**), placing red markers at
both ends of cast-off edge.

BACK AND FLAP

Using 4mm (US 6) needles cast on 83 sts.
Beg and ending rows as indicated and repeating
the 48 row patt repeat throughout, work in patt
from chart until back meas 41 cm, ending with RS
facing for next row.

Place red markers at both ends of last row to
denote top of back section.

Key

☐ K on RS,
P on WS

⊡ P on RS,
K on WS

▱ C7B

▱ C7F

▱ Cr4R

▱ Cr4L

▪ MB

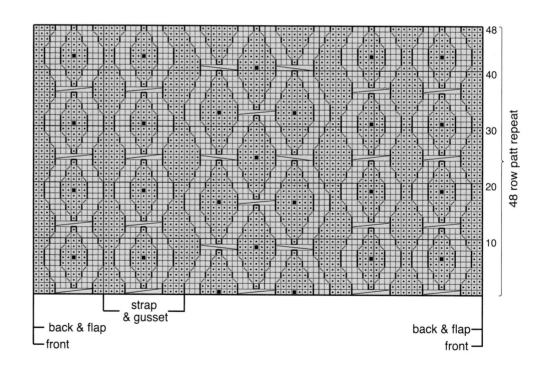

strap
& gusset

back & flap
front

back & flap
front

48 row patt repeat

Cont in patt until work meas 32 cm **from markers**, ending with RS facing for next row. (This section forms flap.)

Next row (RS): K4, K2tog, (K2, K2tog) 18 times, K5.

64 sts.

Change to 4mm (US 6) needles.

Work in g st for 4 rows, ending with **WS** facing for next row.

Cast off knitwise (on **WS**).

STRAP AND GUSSET

Using 4mm (US 6) needles cast on 15 sts.

Beg and ending rows as indicated and repeating the 48 row patt repeat throughout, work in patt from chart until work meas 17 cm.

Place blue markers at both ends of last row.

Cont in patt until work meas 41 cm from blue markers.

Place red markers at both ends of last row.

Cont in patt until work meas 107 cm from red markers. (This section forms strap.)

Place second set of red markers at both ends of last row.

Cont in patt until work meas 41 cm from second set of red markers.

Place blue markers at both ends of last row.

Cont in patt until work meas 17 cm from second set of blue markers, ending with RS facing for next row.

Cast off.

MAKING UP

Press as described on the information page.

Flap edgings (both alike)

With RS facing and using 4mm (US 6) needles, pick up and knit 66 sts along row-end edge of flap, between red marker and cast-off edge.

Work in g st for 2 rows, ending with **WS** facing for next row.

Cast off knitwise (on **WS**).

Join cast-on and cast-off edges of strap and gusset. Placing gusset seam at centre of cast-on edges, and matching blue markers to ends of back and front cast-on edges and red markers, sew gusset section of strap and gusset to back and front. Lay petersham ribbon onto WS of strap and slip stitch in place.

Main image page 15

Berry hat

YARN

Rowan RYC Cashsoft Aran

3 x 50gm

(photographed in Aubergine 017)

NEEDLES

1 pair 4mm (no 8) (US 6) needles
1 pair 4½mm (no 7) (US 7) needles
Cable needle

TENSION

19 sts and 25 rows to 10 cm measured over
stocking stitch using 4½mm (US 7) needles.

SPECIAL ABBREVIATIONS

C7B = slip next 4 sts onto cable needle and leave
at back of work, K3, then P1, K3 from cable needle;
Cr4R = slip next st onto cable needle and leave at
back of work, K3, then P1 from cable needle;
Cr4L = slip next 3 sts onto cable needle and
leave at front of work, P1, then K3 from cable
needle; **MB** = (K1, K1 tbl, K1, K1 tbl, K1) all into
next st, turn, P5, turn, K5, lift 2nd, 3rd, 4th and
5th sts on right needle over first st and off
needle.

HAT

Using 4mm (US 6) needles cast on 102 sts.
Row 1 (RS): K2, *P2, K2, rep from * to end.
Row 2: P2, *K2, P2, rep from * to end.

These 2 rows form rib.
Cont in rib until hat meas 11 cm, ending with **WS**
facing for next row.
Next row (WS): Rib 2, *rib 1, (M1, rib 3) 3 times,
rep from * to end. 132 sts.
Change to 4½mm (US 7) needles.
Cont in patt as folls:
Row 1 (RS): P2, *P2, C7B, P4, rep from * to end.
Row 2: *K4, P3, K1, P3, K2, rep from * to last
2 sts, K2.
Row 3: P2, *P1, Cr4R, P1, Cr4L, P3, rep from * to
end.
Row 4: *(K3, P3) twice, K1, rep from * to last
2 sts, K2.
Row 5: P2, *Cr4R, P3, Cr4L, P2, rep from * to end.
Row 6: *K2, P3, K5, P3, rep from * to last 2 sts, K2.
Row 7: P2, *K3, P2, MB, P2, K3, P2, rep from * to
end.
Row 8: As row 6.
Row 9: P2, *Cr4L, P3, Cr4R, P2, rep from * to end.
Row 10: As row 4.
Row 11: P2, *P1, Cr4L, P1, Cr4R, P3, rep from * to
end.
Row 12: As row 2.
These 12 rows form patt.
Cont as set for a further 8 rows, ending after patt
row 8 and with RS facing for next row. (Hat should
meas 19 cm.)
Shape crown
Row 1 (RS): P2tog, *Cr4L, P3, Cr4R, P2tog, rep

from * to end. 121 sts.
Row 2: K1, *K1, P3, K3, P3, K2, rep from * to end.
Row 3: *P2tog, Cr4L, P1, Cr4R, P1, rep from * to
last st, P1. 111 sts.
Row 4: K1, *K2, P3, K1, P3, K2, rep from * to end.
Row 5: *P2, C7B, P2tog, rep from * to last st, P1.
101 sts.
Row 6: K1, *(K1, P3) twice, K2, rep from * to end.
Row 7: *P2tog, (K3, P1) twice, rep from * to last st,
P1. 91 sts.
Row 8: K1, *(K1, P3) twice, K1, rep from * to end.
Row 9: *P1, K3, P1, K2, sl 1, K1, psso, rep from *
to last st, P1. 81 sts.
Row 10: K1, *P3, K1, rep from * to end.
Row 11: *P1, K3, K2tog, K2, rep from * to last st, P1.
71 sts.
Row 12: K1, *P6, K1, rep from * to end.
Row 13: *P1, K1, K2tog, sl 1, K1, psso, K1, rep from
* to last st, P1. 51 sts.
Row 14: K1, *P4, K1, rep from * to end.
Row 15: *P1, K2tog, sl 1, K1, psso, rep from * to
last st, P1. 31 sts.
Row 16: P1, (P2tog) 15 times.
Break yarn and thread through rem 16 sts. Pull up
tight and fasten off securely.

MAKING UP

Press as described on the information page.
Join back seam using back stitch, or mattress
stitch if preferred, reversing seam for turn-back.

Main image page 31

Mini mobile phone holder

Rowan RYC Cashsoft Aran
    1 x 50gm
(photographed in Oat 001 and Sienna 015)

NEEDLES
1 pair 4½mm (no 7) (US 7) needles
Cable needle
2 double-pointed 3¼mm (no 10) (US 3) needles

TENSION
19 sts and 25 rows to 10 cm measured over
stocking stitch using 4½mm (US 7) needles.

SPECIAL ABBREVIATIONS
Cr4R = slip next st onto cable needle and leave at
back of work, K3, then P1 from cable needle;
Cr4L = slip next 3 sts onto cable needle and
leave at front of work, P1, then K3 from cable
needle; **C7B** = slip next 4 sts onto cable needle
and leave at back of work, K3, slip last st on
cable needle (this is centre st of original 7 sts)
back onto left needle and P this st, then K3 from
cable needle; **MB** = (K1, P1, K1, P1, K1) all into
next st, turn, P5, turn, K5, turn, P2tog, P1, P2tog,
turn, sl 1, K2tog, psso.

BACK
Using 4½mm (US 7) needles cast on 16 sts.
Row 1 (RS): P3, (K2, P2) 3 times, P1.
Row 2: K3, (P2, K2) 3 times, K1.
These 2 rows form rib.
Work in rib for a further 5 rows, ending with **WS**
facing for next row.
Row 8 (WS): Rib 6, M1, (rib 2, M1) twice, rib 6.
19 sts.
Cont in patt as folls:
Row 1 (RS): P6, C7B, P6.
Row 2: K6, P3, K1, P3, K6.
Row 3: P5, Cr4R, P1, Cr4L, P5.
Row 4: K5, P3, K3, P3, K5.
Row 5: P4, Cr4R, P3, Cr4L, P4.

Row 6: K4, P3, K5, P3, K4.
Row 7: P4, K3, P2, MB, P2, K3, P4.
Row 8: As row 6.
Row 9: P4, Cr4L, P3, Cr4R, P4.
Row 10: As row 4.
Row 11: P5, Cr4L, P1, Cr4R, P5.
Row 12: As row 2.
These 12 rows form patt.
Work in patt for a further 2 rows, ending with RS
facing for next row.
Shape armholes
Keeping patt correct, dec 1 st at each end of next
and every foll 3rd row until 11 sts rem.
Work 2 rows, ending with RS facing for next row.
Cast off.

FRONT
Work as given for back until 13 sts rem in raglan
armhole shaping.
Work 1 row, ending with RS facing for next row.
Shape neck
Next row (RS): Patt 4 sts and turn, leaving rem sts
on a holder.
Work each side of neck separately.
Keeping patt correct, dec 1 st at each end of next
row, ending with RS facing for next row. 2 sts.
Next row (RS): K2tog and fasten off.
With RS facing, rejoin yarn to rem sts, cast off
centre 5 sts, patt to end.
Keeping patt correct, dec 1 st at each end of next
row, ending with RS facing for next row. 2 sts.
Next row (RS): K2tog and fasten off.

SLEEVES
Using 4½mm (US 7) needles cast on 12 sts.
Row 1 (RS): P1, (K2, P2) twice, K2, P1.
Row 2: K1, (P2, K2) twice, P2, K1.
These 2 rows form rib.
Work in rib for 1 row more, ending with **WS** facing
for next row.
Row 4 (WS): Rib 6, M1, rib 6. 13 sts.

Beg with a P row, work in rev st st for 8 rows,
ending with RS facing for next row.
Shape raglan
Dec 1 st at each end of next and every foll 3rd row
until 5 sts rem, ending with RS facing for next row.
Left sleeve
Dec 1 st at end of next row, then cast off 2 sts at
beg of foll row.
Right sleeve
Cast off 2 sts at beg of next row, then dec 1 st at
end of foll row.
Both sleeves
Cast off rem 2 sts.

MAKING UP
Press as described on the information page.
Join both front and right back raglan seams using
back stitch, or mattress stitch if preferred.
Collar
With RS facing and using 4½mm (US 7) needles,
pick up and knit 5 sts from left sleeve, 11 sts from
front, 5 sts from right sleeve, then 11 sts from
back. 32 sts.
Row 1 (WS): *P2, K2, rep from * to end.
Rep this row 15 times more, ending with **WS**
facing for next row.
Cast off in rib (on **WS**).
See information page for finishing instructions,
joining front to back across cast-on edges as well.
Fold collar in half to inside and slip stitch in place.
Cord
Using 3¼mm (US 3) double-pointed needles cast
on 3 sts.
Next row (RS): K3, *without turning slip these
3 sts to opposite end of needle and bring yarn to
opposite end of work pulling it quite tightly
across back of work, K these 3 sts again, rep from
* until cord is 127 cm long.
Cast off.
Attach ends of cord securely inside upper edge as
in photograph.

- Our sizing now conforms to standard clothing sizes. Therefore if you buy a standard size 12 in clothing, then our size 12 or Medium patterns will fit you perfectly.

- Dimensions in the charts below are body measurements, not garment dimensions, therefore please refer to the measuring guide to help you to determine which is the best size for you to knit.

STANDARD SIZING GUIDE FOR WOMEN

UK SIZE	8	10	12	14	16	18	20	22	
USA Size	6	8	10	12	14	16	18	20	
EUR Size	34	36	38	40	42	44	46	48	
To fit bust	32	34	36	38	40	42	44	46	inches
	82	87	92	97	102	107	112	117	cm
To fit waist	24	26	28	30	32	34	36	38	inches
	61	66	71	76	81	86	91	96	cm
To fit hips	34	6	38	40	42	44	46	48	inches
	87	92	97	102	107	112	117	122	cm

CASUAL SIZING GUIDE FOR WOMEN

As there are some designs that are intended to fit more generously, we have introduced our casual sizing guide. The designs that fall into this group can be recognised by the size range: Small, Medium, Large & Xlarge. Each of these sizes cover two sizes from the standard sizing guide, ie. Size S will fit sizes 8/10, size M will fit sizes 12/14 and so on. The sizing within this chart is also based on the larger size within the range, ie. M will be based on size 14.

UK SIZE	S	M	L	XL	
DUAL SIZE	8/10	12/14	16/18	20/22	
To fit bust	32 – 34	36 – 38	40 – 42	44 – 46	inches
	82 – 87	92 - 97	102 – 107	112 – 117	cm
To fit waist	24 – 26	28 – 30	32 – 34	36 – 38	inches
	61 – 66	71 – 76	81 – 86	91 – 96	cm
To fit hips	34 – 36	38 – 40	42 – 44	46 – 48	inches
	87 – 92	97 – 102	107 – 112	117 – 122	cm

MEASURING GUIDE

For maximum comfort and to ensure the correct fit when choosing a size to knit, please follow the tips below when checking your size.

Measure yourself close to your body, over your underwear and don't pull the tape measure too tight!

Bust/chest – measure around the fullest part of the bust/chest and across the shoulder blades.

Waist – measure around the natural waistline, just above the hip bone.

Hips – measure around the fullest part of the bottom.

If you don't wish to measure yourself, note the size of a favourite jumper that you like the fit of. Our sizes are now comparable to the clothing sizes from the major high street retailers, so if your favourite jumper is a size Medium or size 12, then our casual size Medium and standard size 12 should be approximately the same fit.

To be extra sure, measure your favourite jumper and then compare these measurements with the size diagram given at the end of the individual instructions.

Finally, once you have decided which size is best for you, please ensure that you achieve the tension required for the design you wish to knit. Remember if your tension is too loose, your garment will be bigger than the pattern size and you may use more yarn. If your tension is too tight, your garment could be smaller than the pattern size and you will have yarn left over. Furthermore if your tension is incorrect, the handle of your fabric will be too stiff or floppy and will not fit properly. It really does make sense to check your tension before starting every project.

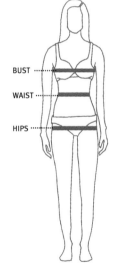

BUST ·······
WAIST ·······
HIPS ·······

BELGIUM
Pavan, Meerlaanstraat 73,
B9860 Balegem (Oosterzele)
Tel: (32) 9 221 8594 Fax : (32) 9 221 8594
E-mail: pavan@pandora.be

CANADA
Diamond Yarn, 9697 St Laurent, Montreal,
Quebec, H3L 2N1
Tel: (514) 388 6188

Diamond Yarn (Toronto), 155 Martin Ross,
Unit 3, Toronto, Ontario, M3J 2L9
Tel: (416) 736 6111 Fax : (416) 736 6112
E-mail: diamond@diamondyarn.com
www.diamondyarns.com

DENMARK
Coats Danmark A/S,
Mariendlunds Alle 4, 7430 Ikast
Tel: (45) 96 60 34 00 Fax: (45) 96 60 34 08
Email: coats@coats.dk

FINLAND
Coats Opti Oy, Ketjutie 3, 04220 Kerava
Tel: (358) 9 274 871
Fax: (358) 9 2748 7330
E-mail: coatsopti.sales@coats.com

FRANCE
Coats France / Steiner Frères, 100,
avenue du Général de Gaulle,
18 500 Mehun-Sur-Yèvre
Tel: (33) 02 48 23 12 30
Fax: (33) 02 48 23 12 40

GERMANY
Coats GMbH, Kaiserstrasse 1,
D-79341 Kenzingen
Tel: (49) 7644 8020 Fax: (49) 7644 802399
www.coatsgmbh.de

HOLLAND
de Afstap, Oude Leliestraat 12,
1015 AW Amsterdam
Tel: (31) 20 6231445 Fax: (31) 20 427 8522

HONG KONG
East Unity Co Ltd, Unit B2, 7/F Block B,
Kailey Industrial Centre,
12 Fung Yip Street, Chai Wan
Tel: (852) 2869 7110 Fax (852) 2537 6952
E-mail: eastuni@netvigator.com

ICELAND
Storkurinn, Laugavegi 59,
101 Reykjavik
Tel: (354) 551 8258
E-mail: malin@mmedia.is

ITALY
D.L. srl, Via Piave,
24 – 26, 20016 Pero, Milan
Tel: (39) 02 339 10 180
Fax: (39) 02 33914661

JAPAN
Puppy Co Ltd, T151-0051,
3-16-5 Sendagaya, Shibuyaku, Tokyo
Tel: (81) 3 3490 2827 Fax: (81) 3 5412 7738
E-mail: info@rowan-jaeger.com

KOREA
Coats Korea Co Ltd, 5F Kuckdong B/D,
935-40 Bangbae- Dong,
Seocho-Gu, Seoul Tel: (82) 2 521 6262
Fax: (82) 2 521 5181

LEBANON
y.knot, Saifi Village,
Mkhalissiya Street 162, Beirut,
Tel : (961) 1 992211 Fax : (961) 1 315553
E mail : y.knot@cyberia.net.lb

NORWAY
Coats Knappehuset AS,
Pb 100 Ulste, 5873 Bergen
Tel: (47) 55 53 93 00
Fax: (47) 55 53 93 93

SINGAPORE
Golden Dragon Store,
101 Upper Cross Street #02-51,
People's Park Centre, Singapore 058357
Tel: (65) 6 5358454 Fax : (65) 6 2216278
E-mail: gdscraft@hotmail.com

SOUTH AFRICA
Arthur Bales PTY,
PO Box 44644, Linden 2104
Tel: (27) 11 888 2401 Fax: (27) 11 782 6137

SPAIN
Oyambre, Pau Claris 145, 80009 Barcelona
Tel: (34) 670 011957
Fax: (34) 93 4872672
E-mail: oyambre@oyambreonline.com

SWEDEN
Coats Expotex AB, Division Craft,
Box 297, 401 24 Grteborg
Tel: (46) 33 720 79 00 Fax: 46 31 47 16 50

TAIWAN
Laiter Wool Knitting Co Ltd, 10-1 313 Lane,
Sec 3, Chung Ching North Road, Taipei
Tel : (886) 2 2596 0269

U.S.A.
Westminster Fibers Inc,
4 Townsend West, Suite 8, Nashua,
New Hampshire 03063
Tel: (1 603) 886 5041 / 5043
Fax (1 603) 886 1056
 E-mail: rowan@westminsterfibers.com

U.K.
Rowan, Green Lane Mill, Holmfirth,
West Yorkshire, England HD9 2DX
Tel: +44 (0) 1484 681881
Fax: +44 (0) 1484 687920
E-mail: mail@ryclassic.com
www.ryclassic.com

For all other countries please contact
Rowan for stockist details.